The World Before Snow

The World Before Snow is Tim Liardet's tenth collection of poetry. His third collection, *Competing with the Piano Tuner,* was a Poetry Book Society Special Commendation and was longlisted for the 1998 Whitbread Poetry Prize. *To the God of Rain,* his fourth collection, received a Poetry Book Society Recommendation, and *The Blood Choir,* his fifth, won an Arts Council England Writer's Award as a collection-in-progress, was a Poetry Book Society Recommendation, and was shortlisted for the TS Eliot Prize. Liardet was awarded a Hawthornden Fellowship and has reviewed poetry for *The Guardian, Poetry Review,* and *PN Review.* He was Poet-in-Residence at *The Guardian* and Visiting Poet at the 2008 Internationales Literaturfestival Berlin. He has performed his work on BBC Radio 3 and BBC Radio 4 and has been translated into Farsi, Macedonian, and German. *The Storm House,* his eighth full collection, a book-length elegy for his brother who died young and in mysterious circumstances, appeared from Carcanet in 2011. He is Professor of Poetry at Bath Spa University.

TIM LIARDET

The World Before Snow

CARCANET

First published in Great Britain in 2015 by
Carcanet Press Limited
Alliance House
Cross Street
Manchester M2 7AQ

www.carcanet.co.uk

We welcome your comments on our publications
Write to us at info@carcanet.co.uk

A CIP catalogue record for this book is available from the British Library

ISBN 978 1 84777 209 1

The publisher acknowledges financial assistance from Arts Council England

Typeset by XL Publishing Services, Exmouth
Printed and bound in England by SRP Ltd, Exeter

For Jennifer

Acknowledgements

Acknowledgements are due to the editors of the following journals and newspapers in which some of these poems appeared: *Ambit, The Manhattan Review, The New Republic, New Statesman, New Welsh Review, PN Review, The Poetry of Sex, Poetry Ireland Review, Poetry Review, Southwest Review, The Spectator,* and *Stand Magazine.*

'Self-Portrait with Porlock as Laudanum Spook' and 'Self-Portrait as Laudanum Spook Speaking to its Maker' were provoked by the BBC Radio 4 programme *The Person from Porlock,* in which I featured with Paul Farley (prod. Emma Harding, 2012). 'Self-Portrait with Shroud and Radiation Ghost' was commissioned for *Poetry Ireland Review: Name and Nature,* 112 (ed. John F. Deane, April 2014). 'The Guam Fever' appeared in the anthology arising from the initiative *Inspired by Hungarian poetry: British Poets in Conversation with Attila József,* launched by the Balassi Institute Hungarian Cultural Centre to mark Hungarian Culture Day, January 2013. 'Self-Portrait as New Virginity' appeared under a different title in *The Poetry of Sex* (ed. Sophie Hannah, Penguin, 2014). 'Self-Portrait as Water,' 'Self-Portrait with View of the Greater Chihuahuan Wilderness,' and 'Self-Portrait with Opium Den Deep Interior' appeared in *Curator Aquarum,* an anthology for Regina Derieva (ed. Alexander Deriev, Stockholm, 2015). 'Self-Portrait with Flowershop Idyll and Nihilistic Love' was published as a broadsheet by Cambridge Public Library, Boston (ed. Daniel Wuenschel, 2015). 'Self-Portrait with Hiss and Rattle of Sleet' appeared in the pamphlet published by the Cheltenham Literature Festival, April 2015.

Ommerike was the name given to the American mainland by Norseman of the North Atlantic around the beginning of the eleventh century. In May 1972, Shamdeo, a boy aged about four, was discovered in the forest of Musafirkhana—he had been raised by wolves. The English writer Mary Ann Lamb stabbed her mother to death during a mental breakdown in 1976. In 2013 Hans Lipschis, at the age of 93, was arrested for being complicit in the mass murder of Jews at Auschwitz. Crag Jack was Ted Hughes's grandfather.

Thank you to Jennifer Militello at the chequered table in Boston, who took a pile of poems and made them a book; who found the arc I would never have found. *The World Before Snow,* the book and all the rest, would never have happened without her.

Contents

When you come right down to it, all you have is yourself. Yourself is a sun with a thousand fires in your belly. The rest is nothing.

—Picasso

Ommerike

We're told how a flight of grackles and cowbirds
dropped out of the sky in Baton Rouge, thudded
everywhere on the ground, blossomed into gardenias:

the like of light on all that wan and numinous yellow
had never been seen before. A rainbow jetted up
against a pitch black sky. In a single short stretch

of the entire Arkansas river, a million drum fish
flapped ashore. We are not dead, said the fish, we merely
change state, and some prefer to say that we are dead.

You're entering, you say, the new nature in which
anything can happen, where fish begin to swim on dry land
and you and I meet and fall, meet and fall...

this could be something we have done before,
each stoop, each step itself, some form of resumption
though the feet are longer, flatter, the feet are longer,

and what we carry, like a greeting, like old pain
kept in a ciborium that holds it as any sealed pot would,
cupped in our hands like a hawkmoth which beats.

Self-Portrait with Mysterious Figure *as* Coup de Foudre

Sanctus. I could not tell exactly who or what you were,
were not. I thought you might have been the *I, I, I,* of the seabird
seeming to ride out the morning's pale gas, as it seeped, and rose;
or the swathes of light, fretful above the cloud-flown derricks;

or the cloud, see-what-you-will, moving across at such a lick
and seeming to sacrifice itself the minute it was formed
or whatever fugs and currents of the North Atlantic could
reach New York Bay and be lost in its plug-swirl of phosphor;

or the cry vying with truck horn, surge of yell upstaging
the piano scale drifting like time through the open window,
or the motor chug-chugging, the dumped melons trundling
along the wharf as the radio static everywhere seemed to say

that everything was reaching everything—all of these—drawn
into the silence which arches its back and swallows them whole
and mixes them into one, or distils them into the lone figure
standing on the quay, whose hair is blown across her face,

who paces to and fro, and seems to wave but not to wave
and makes the electricity, its charge, its field.

Self-Portrait with Drag-Field and Dark

There was the dark in you, it hung over your features;
there was the dark I saw and recognised what it was;
there was the dark along the eye-line, the wilt of dark

as if it had branded a mark from inside you blindly
onto your forehead, and settled all along your mouth;
it had settled all along your bottom lip, changed its shape,

as if to inflect your countenance however brightly
your hair flashed and you shone. The dark charged
to barter with the dark in me, you belonged to someone else;

you belonged to someone else, and so did I.
We were caught, it seemed, in the star's drag-field
which meant the room very slowly started to rotate.

What began was begun at the dun, customary table
where all things must begin. The id seemed to hug
to the dark that could not be shaken from the head, and dragged

you from your costly peace. Nose to tail, the dark
lay docile at our feet, where we sat and granted one another
the cheekbone of our best profile, lit from the same side.

Self-Portrait with Survivors as Nineteen Selves

But you bring me this wandering-from-the-wilderness
of fractured selves. If it's forty days it's been out there
it could be forty years. It could be the survivors

of the crash, the wreckage left ticking in the heat.
Behind, the dust a ghost skittering up. Look how
the selves idle apart, their clothing torn and stained;

there are eighteen, no, nineteen idling apart this way;
Genefer—with specs half broken, shirt torn at shoulder;
Jenifry—whose brain for all its worth sniffs future wafts

of heat—Jenniver—so *bellicose*, her knuckles raw;
the fourteen others sift from Jenůfa to Ginevra while they
shade a different mood beneath a greenish baseball-peak;

Ginoveva—mildest of all selves, swivels hers around;
she seems uncertain if to stop, or stroll. Or sit.
And this one bringing up the rear—Gwenhwyfar—who took

what all the others could not, and humps the bags;
whose little face is crowned with long, invisible thorns
pressed deep, pressed deep. Who bleeds from her palms.

Self-Portrait with Expulsion from the Garden of Eden

We could have been sinners who found love, and found their painting:
the guilt-ignored, illicit lovers, breakers of the covenant,

the shed and straying ones, who found in one another's hands
like death, but not like birth, the end of separation;

the ones who lived off the savour, not the meat, of the apple,
who lived off the meat, not the savour. The painting of the light

which shoved the sinners out of Eden brought us to it
and we said to each other *it is ours, it is ours, it is ours.*

And when we looked through craquelure and atrium-strains
which lodged as dust might on the high crests of the paint

we felt (with a ghostly shivery sense) all of their despair;
we saw how it was *us*, after all, and had been all along,

we the ones weighed down by the dimensions of the apple,
bent double, or not bent double, beneath the weight of it.

The great light washed them out. The light at their backs—
as we stepped from museum-cool into swathes of heat—

broke on our faces. It bleached us and struck us immediately pale,
stopped us here. Our faces, our feet to the knees, so *white.*

Self-Portrait as Shamdeo Talking to his Future Self

Each fingernail grew like a creature yenning for a new existence,
arched, grew grimy and long, became a kind of implement;

I grew, I cleaved to the muckle of warm wolf-blood
and whatever sort of feather and down it actually was

the filthy nest was woven with—sorrow and ferocity.
Those two old antagonists, so much at odds, both riled

by how much of each they found in one another,
the cast in the eye encroaching like some sort of moon,

snapped and squeaked, and circled. They opened their mouths
as wide as they could but not a single word came out.

There was only their scrapping. And the gasp. In one,
in many, mouths. I could not talk. I was dumb with filthy hands

which bled from the stones, like my soles. Every longest step I took
comprised of tinier steps. You stood me on two feet;

you said, from way way up here, *this is what you see.*
You read to me slowly from the excellent texts;

my grubby finger, its one trimmed nail, caught up with every word;
you taught me to gargle your vowels and consonants

and a mouthful of them both began to make a sound;
I was shocked by—afraid of—the growl of my own voice.

Self-Portrait with Bite as Coral and Jewel

It was my chin into which you sank your teeth,
or was it my shoulder, my cheek or my neck,

or was it my nape's furrow or my bottom lip?
You who had to go way way up on tiptoe to bite—

there was the bite, the bite. Whatever it bit.
By morning there was no swelling or toothmark,

no ring-moat anywhere. Were blood drawn,
it was drawn back in and sent through the body

where it bled to itself. The bite bled inside.
A bite can bite so deep, it can cut in two…

By Wednesday, my left eye began to turn deep green
flecked with amber and scarlet, bespeckled in gold;

my mouth my mouth was gradually changing shape,
my mouth was fuller and somehow grew wider;

my cheekbones first they locked, and then unlocked,
my hands shrunk to half their size, nails painted dark;

my hands shrunk to half their size, half their size
as yours grew bigger and your eyes turned blue.

Self-Portrait as Oxymoronic Love

We like to bite, so fierce that it is tenderly. We mime to wound and tear,
we grip to hold, with teeth. But do not wound or tear or grip or hold.

We like to bite so hard, so tender. We scrabble, we panic, smile
and relax, we balk, enthuse. We energise, withdraw, we make, are new,

there at the gate of being, where we live. It is an oven, a clock,
a thermometer. It is a gate now closed, now open. We will talk the kindly,

ravaged way to ferocity, the blissful walk from fierce, to happy.
Talk has no end, we know, but we talk our way to the end of talk,

gull-gasp with open mouths when nothing comes out at all.
Biting's the new talk. To kiss, to kiss and to bite, at once:

newly budded in want, our teeth that are lethal, are harmless,
are sharpened by want, are blunt, blunted. They scar, draw blood,

those tiny ring-moats are not ring-moats but marks of birth.
I only hate, forgive me, because I love you too much,

now sweet, ferocious-tender, fair and just, now bottoming in grief.
Your hands, diminutive, grow large when they induct

a solace that disturbs the nerve, comfort that bends us double,
reassurance that makes to fret, fretting which becalms. Oh,

we shout, we shout—grow furious—we kiss the shout to sleep!
We bring each other these offerings, one by one. Finding it among

a million smoother and more symmetrical on Einstein's beach,
you have gifted me a lopsided heart, like a stone.

Self-Portrait with Hummingbird as Fingers and Tongue

They might have a ruby throat, black chin, fly vortices,
they might be sleek aquamarine and weigh no more than a penny

and might have wings that whir at infinitesimal speed
as they hover at my ears—your diminutive fingers, your hands—

as if they're drawn by fructose and glucose and galactose
each of which could be sensed, smelt, while something drinks,

something drinks in mid-flight. Your fingers and hands
will hover there in mid-flight at my eyelids, as if little bits could

be nibbled from them when they're shut. So tiny, your hands
could be weightless, or the weight of them lifted by wings

that are so tiny and beat so fast they beat but cannot be seen.
They beat so fast, like a racy heart. They lift the weight

of your fingers until they hover at my forehead, peck;
your fingers, your hands are not heavy, but need the wings to lift them

to my ears, to my eyelids and to my forehead.
Your tongue, your tongue also has wings that beat so very fast,

that blur invisible though the tongue's foregrounded plainly,
it needs the tiny beating wings to lift, to lift the weight of it

until it touches my tongue's tip and hovers there like a beak
tip-tap-tipping on the window, wooing its own reflection.

Self-Portrait as the Tongues of Ellis Island

Speak to me, the way you can, in that embroiled voice
born somewhere way down underneath the Great Hall:
I dreamt it was perpetual water softly bubbling up

and which rose, at source, from the deep pressure below
like a ghost-spring of dialects, at first a pulse:
and now it is what it is, the softest spry crackle

at large in its fluency, like an accord of fractures,
of pain and resilience, indignation and despair,
of joy, of hurt, hope and disappointment, of ache;

its little decibels crinkle into one another to procure
the singsong sum of it. It is your voice—
it is a voice lush as a Rousseau jungle with tiger;

rich as a ballroom interior, lit like an atrium
that drags into view the dark attached to its wheels;
it is the tiger, half hidden, half in brilliance;

it grew out of the soft and multitudinous
and now bubbles softly up, becoming only itself.
It is the threatened tiger. It is the tiger's prey.

Self-Portrait with Badlands and Illicit Lovers

There should be no talk of Job—out there in the Badlands,
where the cracks are bottomless, nothing grows but rock and gulch,

dry soil without root, slick clay, deep sand, dust and stones.
There's no dry grass to blow at all, no shaggy pelt

of anything—and every edge—every starved inch—says
No afterlife. It is the place of many circles where the punished go

to punish, they say, where the masked and primally injured
set out to exact at last the tribal, intimate revenge.

The covenant's smashed. They would surely want
to send us to The Badlands for thoughts such as these.

They will not like, they'd surely hate us, as God does,
for our very special kind of poison, our black sap;

locked together in the embrace we can neither sacrifice
nor break, we hear no hacked or dissenting voice at all;

or we hear a dissenting voice but spoken in what might
as well be Horo or Muskum or Elymian, the spook-minims

of a sound which is merely a sound which seems to ape
the scrape of tumbleweed, beautiful but dead.

Self-Portrait as the Nashua Girl's Reverse Nostalgia

So many times it might have been me, now here, now not;
it might have been me wading waist-deep in cornfield and flat mist,

or uncertain among the pooling firs, now here, now not.
I might have stood in the long coat at the end of your bed

when you woke and could not remember who you were.
Once, you found your way to Nashua, or Nashua found its way to you;

you loved the old mill ghosts, their bleached, half-legible signs;
you loved, through the gap, the Doberman in the fenced yard,

the air timed to sirens as if they brought you home, not home.
You loved this wasteland of flat tyres, copper piping ripped out,

you spent all your time alone, went to the crumbly picture house
and wept alone in the stalls, wept alone. While what you looked like

dated the oafish boy who drove the big machine, what you were
crouched over your desk in the back room, and wrote and wrote:

you can't, you can't make me live like this! you shouted at a life of writing;
as if it were mother and jailer. As if it were father. Or lover.

I might have shown up on the corner, brushed past you in the long coat;
You dreamt—twenty years from this place—the man with the beard

not yet older than you, maybe sitting in some underground station,
and I stood up and walked. You turned your head blindly to listen.

You turned your head to look. You turned your head blindly to see
and I walked in, but did not walk in. I walked in, but did not walk in.

Self-Portrait with Faucet Raised into Red

But this could be looking up at rain, standing still in it as if
whole lakes were drawn up into cloud that could not contain them

and are shed, hiss by hiss, to make a scalding chirapsia
when water—spurts—from a hundred showerheads at once

and makes a fizzing sound which tells us Fahrenheit has a voice;
look up, we say—or do not say—to one another—*look up*,

such rolfing downpour after such a length of life without;
we loom, like giants, through rain and steam, through so much steam

now the faucet's hoiked up into the red, to maximum heat:
this could be a summer storm, thick with mineral smells,

of the grass that steams, thick with new sorts of vegetation.
We do not look up, but find our remote feet through the steam,

the little reddened of a new skin there at the extremities
to which we look down the entire length of ourselves

as far as our toes that seem through steam to be like distant buds,
like a whole body bit by bit emerging from the old.

Were you to look up, throw back your waist-length hair
which is at least three times heavier than normal when it is wet,

it'd make your tiny hands and feet seem even tinier;
and so may you—*look up*—at last, compelled by the showerheads

which slew over your forehead and your shut eyes;
below—your kissed mouth, its mood-verb, new earth.

The Universe as Room Forty-Thirty-Nine

The room is exactly that height from the floor.
Its chairs, on which we sat and faced each other, sit on us.
On us its carpets tiptoe, tenderly, like spirit feet
or the spider of hair cloaking them across.
Its windows look through us, as if we offer a view.
Its sheets throw us off—we stay the shape they left us,
we landed like that when they jumped out of us.
The hotel soap, smelling of lemon, uses us up
and though we are smooth, we get larger and larger.
The ceiling looks up, and reads what we do
as the memory of us moves from one position to another
as if not a single movement is unrecorded
first on rewind, then fast forward, then repeat.
The ceiling rises like heat, until it strikes the sound
of our voices hovering, the bank of all we have said,
the words that seem eager to be said again.
We arc the lock. The key has us make that noise,
that electronic singsong which lets the room in.
The room is exactly that distance across.
Our clothes throw the room, discarded like that.

Ommerike

The snowstorm came down, it blew across Boston,
it said all roads behind you are closed for good;
when mass collides with mass and crawls lower,

when snow falls for forty-eight hours, you have to stop.
It blew. It billowed. Such weight of snow to stop
everything in its tracks. Stop, said the snowstorm,

set out, when I abate, from here. Stop, and watch
the whole of me blow in silence through the glass.
The tumbler knocked from the table by mistake,

it said, is yet to reach the foyer's marble floor.
The body of whomsoever is dumped headlong
will fall but never reach the bottom of the well…

My plane touched down on time, your train was held up
which meant it got in as my plane touched down.
Some fluke of clockwork meant my chronograph ran

as many seconds fast as yours was running slow.
We were booked into the same room by clerical error
under the same name, which was neither of our names.

Self-Portrait as Old House Filling Itself with Furniture

The house, being cold stone, knew better than them how emptiness,
destitute of voice, had a single note which deepened. Only trees

in silence flailing at the windows, like an invocation, like a trance,
only a cloudy-tipped, sixty-watt light bulb attempting to cast

the brand-name on the wall. It was afraid of its own ghosts,
the house, and seemed to dream the latest tenant who saw,

at the other end of the landing, a naked woman standing a moment,
who seemed as she walked towards him about the physics of future,

the sort of storm which followed her. At which stage, shelves
of books rose to the ceiling. A mirror cartwheeled upstairs and flew

to the wall, like the blinds. The great cupboard surged into place,
the couch finagled an impossible space. The bed-frame dropped

onto its iron haunches and thundered like a piano moaning,
settled in inertia. A clear night hatched. The Pleiades slashed

across the rooftop, so intense. The old house, in its own trance,
dreamt her appearance, across the narrow landing, hauled

a whole life into view, up out of past or future, or up out of both,
as if it were wholly attached to her. There were pillows! Pillows,

light as their feathers, falling and falling. They fell where they fell
into their place, her hair on the landing long. The lights in the cellar

came on. Forgetfulness, dreamt the house, will be
cured by forgetfulness. Insomnia by lying awake.

Self-Portrait as the Iago-Cajolement

You want to know? Go in there. Pick the lock of that little hatch
that opens at the back of her occiput. The point of the break-in is

to get in behind what she's thinking. I could of course tell you
but it's best you are the blacked empiricist yourself. So pick

the lock. The hatch'll creak, open. Go in. At first you'll hear the noise
of her iron thoughts moving above you. *Chunter. Chunter. Chunter.*

Do you want to know? Assume it's your right. Above you, her thoughts
will move around like chess-pieces. Or skaters at night. Those blades

cutting arcs and parabolas into the ice, that scouring sound.
There'll be a moment you'll pause to weigh against knowing

the unknowable bliss of not. You want. To know. To find out how
each thought splits open on the next thought as it seems likely

it might or might not disclose what it thinks, until you're lost
in wave after wave of thinking through which you'll get buffeted

towards that empty, backroom cinema of hers
that seems to play on a loop, non-stop. You'll find her

sitting there alone, or the movie theatre sitting in her, the latest feature
playing loudly in her head and her head playing loudly

in the latest feature. Sit some way behind her, so she doesn't sense
your presence. Sit all those rows back in the dark so you can see at last

what keeps her there transfixed, all night. Be sure.
Once you know what you know, you will never unknow it.

Self-Portrait with View of the Greater Chihuahuan Wilderness

From this angle, you can pan over all those cracks in the ground
to zoom in, at very high speed, on the crack in his lip.

So this is the lip-crack itself, close up, roughly in the centre;
it is like two halves of a creviced heart and he lifts his finger to it.

What put him there? Oh, the horrors of the subjunctive.
What began as a *yes it is*, became an *it is not, is not*. As one truth

fell away, to reveal the half-truth behind it, another truth fell away;
the untruth showing through the half-truth showing through the truth.

When he looked at her, he knew he did not know what thought
lay behind the thought, or exactly what might be contained in it.

The wilderness opened. If trust was a crumbly levée
it collapsed and fell in and what poured through it was doubt pure

like air, like sand, like dust. What began as yes *it is trust*
became the wilderness, and he stood on his own out there among

one thousand five hundred square kilometres of uncertainty.
He thought of his thoughts, opening like cracks in the ground;

the extreme temperatures which begin to drop at night.
This may be a desert, but it overflows with wolves.

Self-Portrait with Opium Den Deep Interior

Pain, you are the stifled heliograph which continues to flash,
trying to flash out the brain. You're the text which quivers

Save yourself. Pain, you seem to skulk and mutter and sift
between rib and vertebra a little like Yevtushenko's salt;

you filter, it seems, from ledge to ledge. Pain, you inhabit
the interstices you drop into, like dead things letting go;

you collect in the cranny of oversight, the purlieu of abuse,
in every shrub of shade unreached by recognition.

Pain, you have neither tooth nor claw, but trust at last
in the slow attrition, you wear smooth, like water and limestone.

Pain, you understand the length of the siege. It'll last for years.
Pain, you are beak and worm. The minute one is open

the other is gulped whole. Pain, you do not exist, you are
the drugged bell ringing, drugged forewarning, drugged bulletin,

you are every sorrow that couples with itself, that breeds;
if muscles are shackles, you shackle yourself in them;

you first seal up, then make airtight, the pot of grief;
you dread the solvent which dissolves it away.

Self-Portrait with Flowershop Idyll and Nihilistic Love

Our love licks salt, cracks fleas. Plucks hairs. It knows the name
of each of its organs. Like this. It, being itself obsessive,

has its obsessives stroke the other's face, as if to figure out
what it is they stroke. It augments and it dignifies;

it excites. It, being itself tumultuous, has its recusants shelter
from the storm that clatters in the doorway when there is no storm.

Our love's renunciation. Lawless. Selfish. Hates everything
but itself. Like this. We are lost in the flashmob of blooms.

Attentive to each other, inclined to touch, in our long coats,
we have hands in each other's pockets, hands in each other's hands,

talk in each other's mouths. Our love, being snarly and kept,
misleads the flowergirl; she thinks every word she speaks is heard.

It will, being hungry, have us as victims. It makes its victims not
know
how strange they are, strange to others, not strange to themselves,

it has its victims bear perpetual witness to themselves. Like this.
It, being unkempt, doesn't know, they say, what damage it does,

what grace it earns, advice deletes. It, having a gorgeous smell, is
effluvial
as this green gas, has a smell-less smell like certain orchids. It is thick

as baby breath, like tears inside a particle, particled in summer cumulus,
bottomless as flower-baskets, vacuous as flowergirls;

it, being turgid, in such turgid oxygen, among the lily-tongues,
the most extreme of specimens, bespectacled like this.

Self-Portrait with Thunderstorm and Eschatological Tears

Time for the moil of tearwater warmly to seep through your stones.
Some sampler of God is at work. Time to befriend the animal sob.

For years the tear-duct was a puckered spring, its pinhole
blocked by salt. Gone dry, it gasped, gasped. Forgot what it was.

Soon, the sky will open, storm. The troughs will strop, will fill.
But first, the thunder jumps in the headphones. It leaps and bounces

from speaker to speaker, the thunder talks through them.
This is the oldest logic of shedding, incites your tears as if they are things

which haver and must be called. Time, after so much dry, to wet
the tear-duct, stained by the faintest efflorescence of salt.

Time to weep with a convulsive catching of the breath
and to let every lie, half-truth, every ravage and marring, every harm,

cajole the tear-duct beyond a cramped wont to itch,
in a stranger squall of grace bend you double and make

you sob to the sump. The past will be washed away. Your tears
are hot and necessary, part of the cosmic drama, a smaller storm

but a storm. Be washed, it says, to the after-storm, the smell
of roots. Evolve along with the tear-duct. To the grinning wide.

Self-Portrait as Water

I slide. I find my level always. I am two-thirds you, of everything.
I waver and break. I bid for the whole monopoly, like a spring

not yet reached, like future. The rooms of the future
are the pressure in the spring. They spread their ceilings,

have heightened walls as mobile, as immobile, as water. A wall
is water. You see its sunken currents move. The rooms

are water standing, the windows are filled with snowlight,
with purple thunderheads, a fug of light, whatever's said

in the deckchairs, between those two linked hands.
Water, like a state of mind, bulges and collects at the tap's lip

and its loaded weight clings, swells, quadruples its volume,
wells and wells. One day it will crash, will explode.

Self-Portrait with Goffstown Deep Black and Sun-Up Intensity

Black at its blackest. A town asleep. The only way to walk
deeper into the black where the weatherboard homesteads seem to rise.

I edge, like the blind, down the rainy incline which is a tunnel
channelling one thought to the end of it: leave her in this town.

Leave her among the quiet woods and the saturated grass;
leave her where some say she belongs, give her back her life, her family

and her shiver of trees now shedding their way to cicatrix
in the season she most adores, now black, black-leaved, black-boled.

Such dark can funnel you the decision when its walls are close
so *turn*, right now, turn right now, *turn right now*—to see above the town

such a vast ingot-ring haemorrhage out from the mountains and take
away
your choice. It dents, it stabs, your pupils. It says love

is the havoc at which you cannot balk. Take her out of this place
which holds her, stunts her, neglects her, a million miles from the world;

the sun's further off, over the gulf throbs in furious truth:
it says, know her, you have found her. Take her from this place.

Against the depths of black, it says, this the insistent brilliance:
it burns behind your sternum and it burns behind hers.

Self-Portrait as Borgesian Time

The tyres, hissing away what was. If they spun on the spot they'd be
saying goodbye, hello. They picked up leaf after leaf in the wet

then shed them. A little wooded vision—so perfect—
haloed in condensation—filling each of the wing-mirrors either side—

relinquished, let go. And the two of them intent on the road ahead,
her foot on the gas. The gas burned present, past and future,

the road rose, they considered a little of what will be—what *was*—
the tyres hissed in the wet a little of what is. The trees, the great trees

of russet, tawny, copper—the contest—her most adored Fall.
And it was the long long drive into which she swung the wheel,

at the end of it they found, beneath the trees, the weatherboard house
which seemed itself the trance in which it held them, open-mouthed.

As if once they might have lived here, moved from window to window,
if it wasn't a future place not yet reached. That door. That number.

As if, as they paused in front, the house was trying to be remembered,
anticipated, forgotten. As if it were held there in a single note

which any second might shatter it, disclose what it withheld.
He might have set out from somewhere after the Thirty-twenty
deluges,

she back before the Plague of Frogs. Or from the exact same date
at some indeterminate point, future or past. Or else they seemed to know

as surely as they knew along the way that they would die,
this was arrival, departure, a birth or a death, a birth yet to happen

or a happening a hundred years ago they were setting out for,
the leaves were falling everywhere and they were coming back.

Self-Portrait with Grief-Parting as Shakespearian Precipice

It is a thousand-mile drop. The cliff is stark and physical.
Though sheer, it levels itself out into runways and roads,

what once was a treacherous precipice then is horizontal
and it's the body of the other they hug to with hands, with knees,

with fingers, with bedroom hip and velvet groin, with stomach,
until they're shackled in one another and cling by their nails to their nails

as if either way they might fall, but reach out and scatter
every last shrieking chough below from its cliff-face hole.

As the precipice tilts vertical then rights itself, shuddering steep,
it gives such a view of where the choughs circle in the midway air,

so diminutive; and below, the bottom they dare not contemplate.
He has his arms around her and she has her arms around him

and they will not let go, no, they will not let go, *will not let go*:
and their eyes, so opened wide, bloom tears: they bloom with tears.

They cling together on what's a ledge, a precipice either side
nudged by floes of mist, and down through them, whatever else;

it's hard to tell who it is looks down to a bottom neither sees;
each drops a shoe which will fall and fall, and never reach.

Self-Portrait with Brȳd and Brȳdguma on the Bridge at Dusk

There was no holy vow, no straightbacked priest, just blood
that poured through both of them and the vines that got a hold

of their ribs, and gripped, and tied them invisibly together;
and the roots that bound them at their ankles and their wrists,

and the stalks which yoked them to the other,
the unspoken words which were consumption of the flesh.

They slipped under rite and convention, ground them to dust
between their palms which they rubbed like stones and the dust blew;

and churchly vows, and expectation, and biblical weight, the sash,
and the church flags, the clutch of disapproval, they ground them all

to so much dust like poppy seeds, like resin, like rosin, broken down
to make the sort of powdery white left a little on their palms.

Dusk was coming down and the lights of the Thames and of London
coming up blue and orange and red. Behind, the great dome whitened.

There was no ceremony or word save for the two silver rings
which grew out of one ring, and gleamed in the dusk. They gleamed

in the half-light as if they'd acquired some sort of power
and the whole dusk and the lights took over almost like priest and cowl,

like priest and thurible, and touched their heads, and touched their brows
with such an affirming tenderness of touch, or something did,

and they were startled, elated, and afraid.
Their hearts were butter-lamps tearing.

Self-Portrait with Brȳd and Brȳdguma above the Burning Thames

Wedlock'd in blood and skin, you knew the bridge was the bridge,
the time was Crepuscule. It was the time of shifting light.

It was the time which changes everything. It was the time of make
and shapeshift, and with the light, all else. Change is in the engine,

said the cosmos. And the engine in the light. Below, the river's
in black flames. Walk to the halfway point, stop, look back

at the lit-up dome which seems to be appearing for the first time,
and see how all the city lights are reflected there in your countenance,

as if the whole of London shone itself all over you and had
divested you, but for ghost-veil and braid. You choose a bridge

on which you can don your rings, which gutter and flash, which mix
their storm of molecules as if they are alive. They lead you to where

you'll go, wading strip-lit turquoise, as the lights of Southwark
and Blackfriars come up like a troposphere and their nimbi blotch,

and deepen, and burn through tears, are beautiful, are bountiful,
and not one part of what you see, what supersedes it, outlasts.

God Love the Art Deco Angel

Poor shapeless thing, too shapeless to call a day,
came bumping softly bumping down the stairs.

★

Sequestered in lacquered gold, shoulders a-tilt,
there were two of her waiting at the bottom.
One might have been a mirror, the other its reflection,
eclipsing one another back into one.
The day, if we could call it that, stretched out behind her,
grew long until it was bewilderingly long
and tilted softly from wing-tip to wing-tip
and seemed to have lasted, oh, a thousand years.

★

How she leant, leant into the wind.
If the day was brushed, combed out over Enniskillen
it was knotted over Greenland, became unravellable
over the deepest trenches of the Atlantic,
blown wild over Dalmatia, spindled and tangled
over Newfoundland, over Grand Rapids split-ended…
It deposited him, so to speak, in America;
it deposited him in the foyer armchair.

★

So still, so soft, her gold unseeing light.
The ghost of a drogue parachute blew out
like a brake over each of his shoulders and the day
curled up, snoozed at his feet.

Ommerike

By now we're the practised ones who know
exactly how many miles across the Atlantic it is
and to what sort of depths the trench drops,

and how a thought has feet—how mine can wrap them around
those of your next thought, which wraps its feet around,
which grips so tight, they could be hard to separate.

The toes, the toes of both are interlocked,
they thread through and get behind each other
and we know, so wilfully trapped, how any thought so bound

in cuboid and phalange is much like the haunches
lifted upon the haunches of another thought which grinds
against the pubic bone of it. The two will meet

at a point which is almost halfway across,
or just a little less than half the way across;
a thought breeds another thought which rains

like a rain-at-sea of fingertips along your nape
and one by one they grip like my hands which moistly grip
your hands at the moment yours moistly grip mine.

Self-Portrait with Cylindrical Snowstorm and Tired Pony Playing

The big flakes spindle and churn, they speed up, spin, they eddy
into the windscreen. You drive into the cylinder. What stealth, what hush,

the bore-hole of the snowstorm storming at the fogged glass
out of which two spontaneous angels are blown warm, the headlamps,

slowed down in a kind of churchly respect, that haver, that fracture,
and Tired Pony playing on the radio so intimate and so clear:

I'll love you better than him… This could be my voice, you think,
or a version of it singing these topical words, it could be inside your head,

the voice could be the voice miming to the *diktat* of mine;
we know exactly how the parts of us, complex and diamonded, pour

and collide, expire though in endless supply. The world before snow's
a broken horse. Bony and old. We know only the extremity

of what we feel and what we do, and for us there can be only
these soft collisions, lived life, the more and the more of the road—

The snow's hypnotic. The huge flakes colliding with the glass
scud, are hushed. Your knees are slightly parted and are cold, foot on gas.

The green lights of the dashboard watch you from that angle up
and see you mouth along to the words as my mouth—two, no, three

thousand miles away—also starts to lip-synch, catches up with yours:
…all at once, it's all things all at once… The laden windscreen's

out. The snowstorm's indoors. We submerge in primal descant.
My hot hand touches your forehead. The snowflakes strike my face.

Self-Portrait with Blind-Hounding Viewed in Panoramic Lens

I give the crime to you, I lean my foreshortened hand across and slide
you it like a bowl of fruit, beginning to give off the faintest smell;

like a pot of rusty pins, tied to the pincushion they'll never pierce;
like a thurible of spiked artichokes, a church-plate of wafers

dipped in aloes, a carafe of sour Merlot. And so you see, when I see
the crime in you, it waxes larger and less intolerably tolerable,

and what I play as me-as-victim shows up in this lens, which shows you
always all three-hundred-and-sixty-degrees of mind at work at once,

every thought and its successor, the thought behind the thought,
next move behind the thought, that make it work the way it does

as it goes way behind me and all the way around us, and by so doing
catches me out—the guiltier of my crime you are, it seems,

the more innocent I become. Guiltless, without sin. Your guilt
absorbs the guilt, for two. I do not know this is what I do, I do confess,

and hound you blindly with my furious lack of knowing. This is
a masterclass. The lens like a cold god, like all gods, saying nothing.

It goes round, bears witness in silence but is not judgemental
and knows I scold most the crime I was first to commit myself,

punish more, wish to punish: punish. You do what I have done. The lens
zooms in on the territory marked as FEAR. This is a strange

sort of crack in a continent, full of dark. We will name the crevice,
however deep, however suggestive of crevasse it might seem,

however dark it is, *Blind-hounding*. We will stick a pin beside it
and colour it a colour. Something, say, between yellow and yellow.

Self-Portrait as Sea-Fret and Decompressing Self

Sated with talk, interaction, grief and joy, two-way suspicion—
with nag and sulk, the jealous rant, surge of expectation—

there are times—you must understand—when I have to disappear.
This is a necessary act. I change my body's refractive index

to that of the air so that it absorbs and reflects no light at all and I
become invisible—or else, so much in need of decompression—

surround myself with the chamber into which I vanish and which
is itself invisible. I draw the chamber all around me like a robe

which is invisible. All this interaction makes for altitude.
It is vertiginous, the inert gases dissolve. I have to decompress.

Forgive me. *I love you.* Wait here—in this exact spot—until
I return. I go in old, come out new. I go in frayed and ravaged,

come out new. I go in cooked, demoralised and surfeited
and come out new. I go in old, weighed down, come out young.

When so new, I begin to reappear. It takes—you must
understand—some time. I reappear perhaps a little at a time.

I reappear feature by feature, toe, nose, like someone airbrushed out
from chin to toe, but in reverse, coming back. And when

I come out new, come out smiling, come out happy—you
have worn the already threadbare rug through from the pattern

to the weft, the weft to the shreds. You have worn
through your soles, to your socks. You have worn

through your socks, to your feet. You have worn through your feet,
to the boards. You have worn through the boards. To the waves.

Verte

Slow to wake, or to perceive, concentric
of body and limb, whom you perturbed,
they were big and dumb, these men, they eased you in
beneath the comforter, then held you, wide of aim
and clumsy of touch, they had you there,
you crabbed in their shade, would be awhile
whatever they imagined you might be,
they were chosen after all for mass not mind,
not for the grams they'd never shed in death,
but for the mass against which
you might buffer your excesses, be stopped;

deep pricks or assiduous fictions, it makes no difference,
… and all that mass, more mass than this.
It was my mind, like meat, they fed to the subjunctive
until at the limits of itself it imagined worse:
heathen, lurcher, lickspittle,
derelict, fugitive, tramp, hyena, pigsticker, runt,
the lizard tongue and fairground tattoos
and that collective gloat they shared, are still alive—
If I hated them, I'd love them more for how
they failed, failed to read your intricacy of need;
how they dissolve their atoms into you, into us,
how they hover over us so many at a time like cloud,
those flighty, overweening, heavy-limbed ghosts.

Self-Portrait as Homicidal Love

All those American names appraisingly—two the Gallic inflection
which snuck up. One a little prurient Huguenot or Catalan

which pilfered kudos like bread. One the surname of a two-bit
American actor, who could not act. One the yawn

between light and brighter light. One the phonetic racket
of a schlock trumpet. One a surname shared with the Christian name

of America's most beloved lawman. They splinter and coral, the names,
they elongate like threats, they are the ones who even now

lay claim to you, your body. They trample—are not cut by—
the broken glass which cuts me. They cut, like Neolithic spears,

they bruise like cudgels. The names, like those who own them,
clamour like cudgels. A flash-mob. I did not invite them

or perhaps I did, but either way found myself allowing to know.
A remainder, let's say, of pretenders. Of culprits. A murder

of spent rivals. Of lame suitors. Each one, perhaps, the residue
of the gall. Each one, bidding for the tiniest, pinhead-cluster

of your memory cells. Even the names have bowed heads.
Even the bowed heads are schtick. Even the schtick is dented.

Even the dented, like their syllables, buckled. I invite the men
one at a time to lengthen that dishevelled sort of line,

all wearing the same shirt, so white it is good for positioning
a target. Their belts and shoelaces removed, as they must be. Until

I have them in my sights, the scarlet laser scope projected
mid-forehead, slips towards their hearts the brilliant spot.

Self-Portrait with Tattoo-Ink Galleria and Genderless Being

Gender, you are the odd-eyed tattooist specialising
in tattoos of the Fall on the tongue. The orange ink, the scarlet,

the blue, the seagrass, vermilion, gather on the electric needle
of your nib. They drip like sulphur. Our skin, so thin,

rejects your ink. The thing that billowed and spread under it
tried eerily to show itself, those bits of it not yet coloured-in

suggesting, like Giotto's ghost drafts, an intention
abandoned halfway through. Gender, you would love to get hold

of our bodies. You'd burn us the gridiron norms, the median,
the sacrificial par. It's said your red's indelible, but for us

there are no prompts, no cues, for short-term memory loss,
no hieroglyphs instructing us; like Abelard and Eloise,

we are God's hermaphrodites. We are the gonochorist's
oblivion to anything but possession, and what it seems to want,

how it persuades us to move, to listen to the sounds it makes
and the way in which it plunges and rises, shovels and shoves;

how it wants us to live in one unmarked version of itself
and keep us awhile, where we fly, from the blind, black sack.

Self-Portrait with Nettlebridge as Hunkpapa Lakota Dreamtime

We talked the road to Nettlebridge as we walked it to the roadsign
that pointed down the road. But stopped, we doubled back

through the elm-drips, through web, spider-silk and hacked hedgerow,
where there was everything we remembered, the lane of silt

and rivulet as the night came down, the thorn-glints, the place
where we kissed in the rain and felt it fall, though now much darker shapes,

where we stopped on the way to take the photograph at
the spot that had waited nine months, nine hundred years, for us

to offset its foliage, prop timer on wall, run back to clutch. *Puff!*
Then, the house from where we started out, a single light burning

a smudged yellow and orange, the dull sound of horse hooves on the lane
trundling through its walls, and above the rooftop such a little lot

of stars which seemed to attach itself to the roof-ridge
as if all the constellations somehow belonged only to it…

and further back, bright with madness, the mother behind glass.
All this we remembered, but imagined the Nettlebridge we'd yet to reach

like a grand excess of photons, assembling in the shape of a chair,
while the mother's photons did not assemble her to sit in it.

Or else, when you reach out your fingers to feel for the sharp grass
of how it might read, your hand disappears. Or else, when you try

to step into it in one stride, boot follows hand. This is
what the Hunkpapa Lakota called The Land Yet Without Feet.

Self-Portrait with Dreamwhite and the Ignominy of Dying

Let me hesitate, simper, be afraid, who heard
you speak of your death dream, how you were coming awake,

startled awake, uncloistered in that state, by the thought
of something white exhaling its last exhalation,

a whiteness, simulacrum, a death, you said it was,
a death that made you afraid ever to go back to sleep.

And you wondered who it was died last night, or what
future event happened and made its way back to us in the past

and which, like particles of mist, clung to the hairs of my coat,
to my coat's collar, hem, sleeve, which clung to my hair

like an atmosphere of drench and stealth, that chilled all it soaked
and dragged at my coat-tails as I tried to walk away

to the place where your dream confronted its counterpart:
the cold, the material, shore of the great bed

in which I found her at last—knew that I'd found her—
as tiny as a creature, as weightless a mass so far out by now

among the waves, roiling and backing off and climbing
to kick back against the suck and current that were too strong

as she tried to climb out of nightdress and body
though her chicken wrists held her there, gripped the bed-bars.

Nonagenaria

The bony bowls of her vertebrae
are stacked. They sink into one another
and are grinding her to so much chalk;
when she stoops, her ball-joints
grind chalk-dust out of chalk.

The bowls, the bony bowls
are hunching her deeper and deeper;
they hunch her deeper and deeper
into her clothes, and into her chair,
they hunch her into her body.

And she is drawn, drawn more and more
towards the black hole
of herself, through which so many parts
of her have been lost already,
through which she will be lost:

whatever is left of mind
are a few perished valves, spasm and spark,
the odd breaking down of charge
after charge, transforming
her look and the drop of her jaw.

She is a ghost already, already,
but she is a ghost who keeps
on coming back to this room
to sit in her chair, her deep chair,
and refuse to leave.

Either I can bear the thought
of her sitting in that chair
less than her absence from it;
or her absence from it less than the thought
of her sitting in that chair.

Self-Portrait with Mary Ann Lamb's Arkansas Toothpick

Mother, you lie at the source of the long black river
that does not love the world. You knit black shawls

at the very end of it. Your needles are ivory's shocked white.
Mother, you made yourself a necklace of unthinkable things

which jangle and clash, which knock and witter together;
you bid the Nibelung dwarves come to your knees

and they bob all around you, waiting for you to choose.
Mother, you clamp that caliper around the heads of those

who will travel up the river. This is how you assess them.
You scrooch over your own body like a bird, you pick up

a crumb from your lap. You watch your reflection
in the vague oval and dream it is someone more innocent.

Mother, you laugh, rock back, you have no teeth in your head
which is full of perished veins only, you claim, and little else.

You sit in this room, in the deepest of chairs,
wrapped in your shawls and chair-arms like a sunken fog,

like a ghost with a wide mouth. Mother, when younger,
you turned your head away against a cirrus-blowing sky.

The Guam Fever

after Attila József's 'Belated Lament'

The nurse checks me every hour.

Father, my temperature goes up.

Though twenty years dead
you seem to hover over me, nose to nose:

You never told me the war was over—
and now I'm stuck on this island
in the rags of my body.

You hover, you hover, but I'm so bony-faced
and in this cap so lizard-like
I can only talk, at speed, in lizard-talk…

'Yo… Yo… Yoooosh…'

I'm the sugar-ghost, the glucose-ghost, wading
from the swamps at the jungle's edge…

That arm, only half formed. The lack of thumbs.
That rifle, half melted away. That torso

unforming in the vapours of delirium,
dissolving from the knees down, from the knees up…

the war is over, you say, the war is over,
the war was over long ago;
you place your large palm on my brow.

About to break my sword,
about to break my vow and break my word
I have shed the debris of my army boots

and slipped back
into my boiling,
no, my icy feet.

Self-Portrait as Truth-Houdini and the Chinese Torture Cell

The chains and the tank and the water and the crowd,
my petite soubrette, the all and the all, all these. The mineral taste

of the water and the chains upon my skin like a cruel kiss,
like cruel fathers, like steel, like steel. The goosebumps like

a million needles excited. Or a lunatic's yen for ogling.
The escape that locks up with me then liberates the multitudes,

frees me from gender, hair-shirt, Hungarian lisp. Dear Bess,
my feet are shackled in stocks. I am suspended in mid-air,

I am locked in underwater. Is this a terrible cramping of limbs
or birth in water? Am I a drunken man staggering, or do I

merely carry a heavy weight upon my back? Is it my face
that g-forces upside down underwater, or not,

my slow hair that blooms trying to escape the face?
The tank's inertia, brutish-physical, chains the cruellest physics,

the water cold, the lungs never meant to drink, cheeks to puff,
neck muscles to protrude as if they might burst. Oh, what

of shackling truth can mind and body finagle a way out of
and burn up. Water is cold, but this is not water. Chains are steel,

but these are fraught saviours. Stocks bruise skin, these are cocked saints;
a lisp is a thing for mocking, but this is royal blood. A hair shirt

itches on the inside, but this is dreamt meadow. I am not
alight. These are not flames rolling over my body.

Self-Portrait as Truth-Houdini at the Confessional Grille

It wasn't me, Father, though you think it was. Not me. I never said
what it seems you think I said. Nor did. No. You must try

to believe me. The want, you see, is in your trust. Your mistrust,
if allowed to be a dog, will it come to its master with both its ears down,

exuding human guilt at the smell that something else has made,
all wagging flaccid, limp? All three hundred million of its scent-glands

convinced, because they twinge and lug, they can smell lie;
can smell pheromone, gender, mood, smell a shift in atmosphere

and now, above all else, the lie. The scent-particles are gathering
on the nostrils of your mistrust! Your ear at the grille.

If one side of it there is a voice talking, the other side is silence
drawn down into its sediment. I know you think that truth, for me,

is a slippery hand-hold with metaphor. They then let go.
I was three, you guess, when I first looked down at your toe-cap

and tackled a fib. The fib sprouted. Speaking, it taught me how a world
can tilt up different in a glimpse. But no, it was not me,

you're tall and strong. Lift me up by the ankles and let whatever is
in my pocket clatter and rain on the stones of the courtyard

to clinch or exonerate, crowd me into a much tinier space.
These pockets turned out, my shirt undone and extended either side

like wings, I show you who I am, and click that moody hound of yours
to come curl up at my feet, be stroked, however much it squeaks.

Self-Portrait with Prayer as Stupidus for Continued Sobriety

Trashed, Lord, I was as crazy, as off-with-the-angels as Harpo
about to smash up his piano to find a harp. Having no hair, there were

as few intelligent words as curls. I was lost back in a time
before language was invented. But without it, Lord, the firewater,

the hooch, the sauce that frees up the wrecking, inhibited tongue,
the mouth gets smaller and smaller. Poor mouth. It is a purse

without coins. A puckered ass-hole. It begins to take smaller sips,
speak smaller words. It is obsessed with getting its tongue

around the speaking of smaller and sweeter, sucked-tiny words
around which it fits like a clam. Look how very small, how very tight,

the mouth becomes. So small, at times, it seems it could
be about to disappear. A Magritte-sky flows through the mouth

that almost isn't there. It is neither pleased, indifferent nor glum.
Poor tongue. When there's less of mouth, there's less of attitude. Sobriety

is a little like being held down and force-shaved of your own beard
to discover beneath the thinness of the lips, the hole through which

not a drop will pass. Everywhere, drinkers crowd in. When they smile,
when they grin, their incisors are blood-red. Beneath the beard,

there is the person you have yet to meet, or name. Any loose talk
of Truman Capote's liver plummets through the evening

like a stone. Sp-splash! To mention it's as if you sneezed yourself
a social allergy. Guilt, like some sort of hackle, is wheezed.

Hemingway drank, and had his gun. When the leery consensus
looks back at me, I fear I might have turned it on myself, and squeezed.

Charm Against the Dandelion Wine

You did not teach me, Lord, did not teach me how
six or more buckets filled with the florets
of your otherwise placid flowerhead
plucked from the deep shadow of the yellow meadow,
when mixed with lemons squeezed for sap,
with raisins, with water and sugar, bled
with potassium and yeast into the slop and slap
of all of these bubbling up to heave off
the lid of the fermentation trap

would turn me, Lord, turn me at length
into the sort of wreck any friend or relative would
be embarrassed to prop up in public,
any tent-pole refuse pow-wow, guest translate
such mawkishly loving gibberish;
a wreck which, when attempting to piss, would lurch
forward and be pitched straight
down the dark fern-bank, flailing with hands outstretched
back towards dirt and a handful of root.

Ommerike

When we struggled, or dowsed, for our first words,
when we sat at the table and traded charm for lowered eyes
and found ourselves so far up in the light of the room,

when our two-way curiosity was like a stick that twitched
and something seemed to have left its primitive breath on our glass,
way down, let's say, way down, way down in the river

which flowed beneath the thoroughfare of Fifth Avenue to round
the bend in Minetta Street to the north-east, Bleecher Street
to the south-west, and which from time to time, given its mood,

might show itself roaring at grates, send up a certain smell,
or flood the very lowest level of the elevator shaft to five feet,
or rise first into the laundry room, then the library cellar,

always leaving a spiky efflorescence in the plaster before
dropping back to do what it did best, heading on under—
when we leant across, way up in the light, way down there we rose

from the river's surface at the same moment, seemed to form
by rising, the cloudy mirror into which we smiled.
Is it you? I asked. And you replied Is it you?

Self-Portrait as the Sarawak Bats Addressing Hans Lipschis

We of the wrinkle-lip, wing and hand, we of the cackle and tooth,
who make the tide engorge and bulge from the cave, who swarm it

wide and high, who turn it, at its furthermost extent, back
into the cave, we are your sins. Who swarm out into the last of daylight

as if we're night itself, rolling up the light. We do this every day
at exactly the same time. Old man, we do not grow old,

we stay the same age, your sins have faces. Regard us, zoom
in on our features, that tiny mincing mouth, those eyes that are so small,

too small to be eyes. We feed, are fed upon. We are your sins,
we multiply. Our tongues, if we have them, are black, our teeth leak.

Our hearts are a million black flowers pulsing, pulsing and opening,
they pump and urge, they fetter and strive, we are your sins

and are much alive, now two million strong. Old age cannot
unload its sins. We breed in a rank darkness and chivvy

a million squeals to make power. Our fingers are tiny replicas
of the hands with which you did what you did, you might yourself

have wrapped around the neck of every Jew who died.
We hang upside down in the cave, we mass in a roofspace

into which three Nuremberg rings could be fitted, one by one
we are like the particles of the primal darkness spreading over,

its thrilled hearts, its Geiger-counter energy ribbed. We are
the schleppers, the luggers of the murdered thousands, we smell the milk

of repentance. The wide tide of us clouds and billows at dusk, it wants
to raise you from your death-bed and lead you to the glass.

Self-Portrait as Hans Lipschis Addressing the Sarawak Bats

If I pause, vagrant, wear a soft chemise, prove
so slow my interlocutors must sigh, suppress impatience, glance at watch,

decide a deaf nonagenarian deserves no accusation such as this,
you must forgive me. You devils of my light and day,

of the pantomime ears, I am old. The ailing one who'll hobble
and never in this lifetime straighten his back. Bring an old man

his blanket. There are your many bodies massing and squealing,
casting darkness all over me. My liver's a stone. My heart a mess

of misfires, the right ventricle dwarfed by the bloated left. And my brain
lopsided, vein-swollen. My left eye slackly magnified, like fish-scales,

my bones ungainly. The knuckle-joints lock, stay stuck. I am too old
to be a sinner. My duodenum rattles. Be sad. My sins are not

this daily flight of devils at exactly the same time, but pups
in a basket, sniffling. Or dragging at the teats of a long-dead mother.

The murdered thousands thread through me, like children, reach
for my cuffs, and tug their accusations. They have been forgotten

and at length, I have seen it in a dream, I'll be the one who'll thrash
down some sort of a chute to a death, without a single tooth

or thought in his head, more a twitchy cadaver than anything else,
sucked into the vacuum of madness where nothing worldly calls

but these gradations of dispatch, these increments of farewell:
look, his chin and collapsed mouth drawn in an almost comedic grimace,

he knows whatever he has done will be forgiven, appeased, solved,
sanctified. The dead die with him. He recalls, he remainders, nothing.

Self-Portrait with Porlock as Laudanum Spook

Laudanum was my blood. Its very particular work the smile.
My blood was laudanum. My body in repose—supinely,

gleamingly—my elongated arms a roust to catch a hold
of the darkness—became the smile. At first, thrown back, it was

strange I should have dreamt so large a dream and at the same time
dreamt the means of scuppering it. I dreamt the laudanum spook

—so tall, perhaps seven feet seven, turning his brim in his hands—
he, or perhaps I should say It, stooping out of the light

as I opened the door, though there was no door. No knock.
The knock was already indoors, sulking. It was waiting for something

to hang a hat on it. The knock was the next thought,
looping. The knock was the drought of the ink. The thought-drought.

The knock was the drug-sweat, allowed to break. To quicken.
Whoever, or whatever, it was that stooped as it did was everyone's

picked, intercessional figure. He was the one who trafficked
the excuse. It was the sabotaged dream with the saboteur

gashing its hull. It was the hull with the gash, nonetheless setting out
for the destination it could never reach. And I knew,

as did Porlock, the vision was flawed in the first place. I have come,
he seemed to say, as ruiner and saviour. I have come, he said, he stooped

smiling all the way towards me and I sent him out at last
to visit the rest, to not-knock when they most need him.

Self-Portrait as Laudanum Spook Addressing its Maker

The chemicals surge—are your blood—are the rattle and swell
of your corpuscles. Your blood is thick—is thick

with laudanum—speeds, then slows. The pain-switch, so to speak,
is thrown. I seem to grow out of the morass I wade

which might at the very second that it reaches my knees
be attempting to erase me. I grow ganglier and eerier

first out of glucose-want, neglect, fat and acid, then the drug,
and I grow and I grow until something abnormally tall,

the very thing of your own making, the excuse, the plea,
the alibi, the stall. The alibi for every failed commission,

every stunted *Kubla Khan*. Every drug-induced forgetfulness,
every search, on returning, for something more easily blamed

than the self. I am the dubiety which grows tall,
grows feet, nose, large hands, long neck, pinpoints for eyes,

and you have me knock at the most importunate, most
convenient, time. The knock of the knock! That burst vessel

in your left eye spreads like a country. *Wreckage!* The more
I come to meet your need, the realler, more plausible I become,

a strangely elongated stranger calling about a horse.
Ah me. When I'm the very trance you founder in, you think I am

Golgotha in outsized boots, frazzled hat, who'll take all the blame,
redress the squander. I should have killed you before you killed me.

Self-Portrait with Shroud and Radiation Ghost

It's estimated tens of millions of volts were required
to burn the willowy ghost into the cloth. It was the radiation

scorched into the raw herringbone where it fell in its folds upon
the features of a man: here where the bony knee-joint

was slightly raised, here the bruised eyelid, the line of the mouth
and hands which rested gently in the groin—I want to touch

the weft of the cloth, hold it to my cheek in its forty-eight folds,
place a finger through each hole where the boiling incense dripped

through the mite-infested fibres, and smouldered a hole,
found nothing at all the other side. As my finger pushes in first

through this hole, then this hole, then this, whatever percentage
of it passes through, disappears. Withdrawn again, it is whole.

The burns—the charred marks—of thermal radiation take a second
to form, a second, a thousand years, to disappear. The burns

are disappearing into the dark cloth. I want to lift it,
to hold it to my mouth to see if it is rough, or soft, or if it drops

to ash. To ash. Though palpable, the image is precarious
and not light-stable. As the cloth around it which remains uncharred

darkens as if to merge into night—though science tries to drag back
the scorched ghost, though I half try to hold it, half let it go—

though mouths which were emptied of them
now fill with ashes—though the Atheist starts to speak once more

in the first person plural and my father twenty years dead
must die once, die twice—all we have's a ripped rag.

Self-Portrait as Homo Erectus

All is slovenly smash up. We don't live long. Things are solved simply.
The grimace, it gathers. The grimace breathing steam on the mirror

and the grimace breathing back. To all broody acolytes, we are
the ear in which to whisper incitements. We follow one another

through our pain, our pain. We lift weights, touch knee-to-knee, watch
ourselves lift weights… If every quiver's matched by every quiver,

every flushing up is twinned with every flushing up. The grimaces
all but kiss. Their eyes could be looking for fleas. There are the shakes

and the shakes, that grunting away of pain and the grunting away
of pain which confers on us, we think, some stature. Not for a second,

not for a single second do we let up on this stalking at close range
of the swollen clone in the mirror, through which, it seems,

devoted and devotee drink from the same straw, break bread, grunt.
Only we descend as far as floor and ankles will permit us to, then rise

to the full extent of ourselves, in exact unison, our neck muscles
straining, straining. So having seen us once, you must see us again;

this is the glass, the glass that is merely integument, a skin;
we have to have the glass to make sure we're still here. Where's law?

There's only physique, and its shackles. We suffer bad dentistry,
walk on foot, could smash a head open with the femur of a deer.

Grunt

'Well... tell you what. Curley's like a lot of little guys. He hates big guys. He's
alla time picking scraps with big guys. Kind of like he's mad at 'em because he ain't
a big guy. You seen little guys like that, ain't you? Always scrappy?'
—John Steinbeck, *Of Mice and Men*

Your foot shy of the rowing machine's baggy loop left by Babe Ruth;
his feet twice the length, three times the width,
that big toe, the left one, an embarrassment.
He was six-two, weighed two hundred and fifteen pounds;
his arms would have reached around you twice.
What he had in body, though, you make up for in subtlety,
in charisma, in wit and in charm, you think,
even though a hundred pounds lighter, even though five-eight;
when you row you grunt, as if to inhabit one bigger,
as if the bigger grunt might propel you like a sail.

It goes on, the war between big and littler men.
Okay, you say. The ghost goes through its work-out.
For its every long pull on the oar—from shin-bone to waist—
you have to pull five or more to keep up with the pace.

Self-Portrait as my Grandfather Lip-Synching to Crag Jack

I must beg forbearance for the quality of the recording
which keeps my voice like a distant thing however much I raise it,

like a song in a storm of interference, too small against the storm:
the old black prison that hung over the valley and whose walls

were always running with wet, whose steep slates gleamed
and whose chimneys rose so high—I was locked, locked up, in there;

I was locked inside the iron gates and locked within the walls
and was the only one, they say, ever to tunnel out of it,

to claw my way up to the long, mannerly and dewy grass:
and that's how you seem to have me on your clean pages,

tagged between the covers of your books, grimy in half escape;
I seem, as you have me, to break out but never actually to break out,

to come up with mouthfuls, with pocketfuls of earth,
with peat and clay beneath my fingernails, my broken fingernails,

and stones spat out of my mouth. Do with as you will—
my clumsy common man lurch, my broken features and ripped coat

strike something in you but strike very little in me
as I surface from underground again, but never get out—

the light beaming down through dark from the high guarded wall
catches the whites of my eyes, before I go back down.

Self-Portrait as Crag Jack Lip-Synching to my Grandfather

All my life I've been locked up. There were walls between me
and your books, between my broken fingernails and your pages;

walls between me and worldly wealth, and the means to make it;
between me and the uplands, between me and whatever else might help

to straighten up my back, at last. I sat where I sat,
and was never far from that single shaft of light which seemed

to furrow my brilliant frown, so bright I had to close my eyes;
how it showed every fold, every stage by which a face had grown

too large for the person who inhabited it, one magnified eye
slackly blinking. A man slow of mind, but strong of arm, always

has to stay where he is sent, through the swung gate, the lock.
Not for me the scrape scrape scraping at the three-foot-thick walls

with the tines of a pilfered fork, worn away until all but toothless.
I was squaddy, stoker, a feeder of history's flames; I was

two hands greatly for labour, a drunk, oh so often was I found
where I dropped, yes—I was all of these, all of which kept me inside;

while others attempted escape, I stayed, was as much withdrawn
into the corner of my cell as of myself until such a time

the prison doctor shone his little flashlight down my throat
to whatever it was he saw, pink if it was pink, maker of a voice.

Self-Portrait as New Virginity

I was thrown, you might say, on the mercy
of her knowledge. Were there less, there'd be plenty:
undo this, she softly cajoled, no, *this*.
Miles away, her slant green eyes slid up
to the contingencies of cloud ebbing over the sidings.
When she wrote it there on the subway wall
in an unbookish hand as deep red as Chianti
she dropped, as she dropped her gaze, the *r* and *i*—
X marks the spot. Here's where the mammer's boy
lost his viginty.

It, like something uncoupled, indeed was lost
along with the cart of old dogs and dead haloes,
along with all sense of ingenuous folly
once the chemicals started to boil in the pit.
It was lost there, or left, or merely discarded
like creaky, unbroken shoes, like out-of-season holly.
It was lost, or merely dumped
along with everything else no longer of use
down at the deep end of *Viginty Alley.*

Self-Portrait with Rhode Island Spontaneity and White Light

Shadowless, tidal, to make white every obstacle,
every edge, every curve, every biscuit-jar. As if, say, as much a mist, a fret,

a steam, as if as much an infinitesimal fine white dust
of photons shed on every surface, the white light—you mime—

fills the house in the morning, the light which is soft and thick
fills the whole of the spacious kitchen but does not make you squint—

What is white, is made whiter. What is not white is made white.
It's as if you are wearing earpieces so you can hear me talk

but do not talk back, you mime. You gesticulate, you draw
your clues upon the air a surrogate for words. Those lips,

your whole mouth, rests—this, I realise, is how your mouth rests.
I can more fully see it when at rest, your eyes, your whole face

the light brings to refulgent blazing all down one side
like a lopsided halo, catches cheek, the way your face prepares itself to smile

while I provide the commentary, you listen, you mime.
From here, I cannot hear the waves, collapsing on the shore

but maybe you can, both touchable, and beyond touch.
The white light is clean and clear and bright and makes everything shine

when it is everywhere all around you like this. You know
this is the way that the ocean rarefies its form. I can read your mime.

This is the way, if I read right, your tiny hands reach up
and seem to touch the light itself, the way the ocean comes indoors.

Self-Portrait with Water-Dry and Laws of Probability

Which means, I continued, my train had to break down
in the extreme north of Uttar Pradesh and offer up in gasps

the one-in-seven-hundred-million chance I'd run into you
sitting beneath that ceiling fan, turning your glass in your fingers

a thousand metres from where the engine stopped
ten miles from Lucknow, five thousand two hundred and eighty-two

from that rainy English town and place of learning that
fastened itself to the both of us like a clam, its moss in our socks...

Because so unlikely, you replied, dependent on
the variables of time and space, quanta, the heat

and number of people strolling down the track set against
the number leaving the tea room and at what rate;

because it was dependent, you said, on
exactly how long it took you first to blow cool, then drink your tea,

how long it took me to stroll back down the track;
because it depended on the vagaries of metal fatigue

that meant the crankshaft of this old blustering Lister
decided like a peevish animal it had had enough of work

at that exact moment, that angle of the sun;
because it depended as much upon the time it took the one of us

to ease down from Kashmir on bus and bike at that rate
to this mozzie-infested station, the other to edge

his way towards it across the Great Syrian Desert at that speed,
Oh yes, you said (...looking up and grinning subversively

beneath your wide mathematician's hat),
it was all but impossible to avoid each other.

Self-Portrait with Hiss and Rattle of Sleet

Not frogs, not grackles or cowbirds, but sudden and tumultuous,
sleet—we're the only place for miles around, it seems, where sleet

does not fall: sleet hammers on, slides off, the umbrella, makes a space
that is dry. As much as it fizzes on the countryside, road

and every square inch we can see, it makes for us this space
in which we stand, hunch, lean-to, in which we huddle together

to watch sleet get more boisterous—it reaches our extremities,
it gathers like snow on our sleeves, our backs and our shoulders,

out in it: mesmeric. Compulsive. The way those little cuticles of ice
clatter and blitz, sizzle and rebound, parabola and skip.

Each one contains the storm. They jig and leap. In slow-mo and real time
they act out their crazy ballet of expenditure like grapeshot,

pure pelletry, like blasted grains. Like maggots bouncing, you say,
they all come down and try to find themselves a little home.

They fizz and crackle, don't last long; it is their death-dance—
We huddle close, are strangely indoors, and can hear how sleet

can blast itself against the road and somehow make a tender sound.
There is more than rib and nylon between enfilade and dry,

between the road and the clouds. We talk with big voices to drown out
the hiss and rattle of sleet by which our voices are drowned out.

Self-Portrait with Turgid Blossom and St Paul's Stooping

When everyone else in the city was bolt upright and walked
we lay beneath an awning of blossom sieving light. The sifter of blossom

shaking and sieving above us. And through it—sky.
And through it—scud of cumuli. This horizontal version

of upright. People walked past us loomingly at odd angles,
hurrying, full of the leaning towards. The great ethereal dome

stooped, through the blossom. We lay out on our backs
in our long coats which reminded us it was March and cold,

cameras in hand, in its roseate light. Your face, your mouth,
beside me in the lens—smiling so huge, up close. Each blossom

was a peacock's eye—encased in pink, an encrimsoning clue,
a lens through which to scrutinise the wan presence of St Paul's.

Hello, you say, *us in the future.* Where we lay out
beneath blossom-boughs which nudged and elbowed, and bumped.

So much farther back—farther forward—all of this goes on and on,
your mouth opens towards me, dome stoops, the light's cast over us

beneath blossom-boughs which nudge, and elbow, and bump.
As if all these petals, so many of them, had

been retrieved where they fell and trodden barefoot into a turgid pulp
of a brandy to be consumed, we drink ourselves.

Self-Portrait with Flames and Arapaho Bison

We should have taken better note of what crashed through the wall,
what primal animal force, head ducked, what near-extinct species

which can cross any river more than a mile wide from what to whatever;
what force when drought-moulted, when smelling water,

sets a thousand like it running. Stuffed, it froze as it crashed.
In the bar beneath, though we hardly knew it, we were more taken

with the smell of burning, more taken with the flames themselves
—the bus back, burning in the black of the snowfield—

which might well have been the smell of preconception in flames,
the smell of chance, like rubber, burning. The smell of discretion,

like kerosene, burning up, then tearing in the wind. The smell
of neglect, like the stuffing of seats, burning. The smell

of stagnation, like the nap-pile over the crankshaft, burning.
We fed the flames with the detritus and napkins of weddings,

a marquee's striped canvas, doilies, whatever stuffed collapsing thing
sat upright for a while in the flames and then fell forward.

It is my conviction that night that we were burned alive,
for the briefest minutes you sat opposite, you flexed, you flailed,

you grinned so wide, you seemed like me to be fuel for flame,
all we'd been was eaten by flames which lengthened, which blued;

we stood up in flames that burned us alive but could do us no harm...
Above the bar like a train, or an engine stuffed with time, while all

those flaming Arapaho arrows skidded off its back the clumsy bison
crashed through the wall, we stepped away from the flames, the past.

Self-Portrait with Aquarium Octopus Flashing a Mirror

Where water, glass and light cut through each other, where one side
of the glass is underwater and the other is not, one cosmos

seems first to bisect, then kiss, another. Up against the steamy divide
the octopus explodes and collapses, explodes and collapses

in its soft hysteria of saying: it is compelled by will or ennui to be
wholly on display, compelled, like any extraterrestrial, to show itself—

This is what I've got, it says with every lunge, I'll show you all I've got
which you don't have, this head, for example, clumsily bashing glass

like a blunt-nosed angel's, a throb of plasma. Though many limbs flower
crazily from this eye-lens, it says, I don't know what it is I've got

but here's the centre, the centre where it is. And you a man, a woman,
it says, and you neither or nothing at all—a smudge in need of an apogee.

You don't know what I am or what it is you are, you do not know,
whatever you are, whatever you are, whatever you are.